A SHAKESPEARE ACADEMY
PRODUCTION

This book is dedicated to the memory of
Dr. Jan Gillquist.
1934-2016

Jan was a deeply cultured man, who in addition to his scientific achievements—an orthopaedic surgeon famous worldwide for his research into sports injuries—was an artist, musician and horticulturalist. He and his wife, Karola Messner, were active supporters of the Shakespeare Academy. Their perceptive and challenging commentaries on our posts were a constant source of inspiration, and we greatly valued their serious and dedicated approach to life.

Together Jan and Karola created a 6-acre sculpture garden at their home on the Baltic Sea, which contains over a thousand roses and almost as many rhododendra. Their finest garden, however, is the relationship they cultivated together over many decades, and it is as a devoted, dauntless and original couple that we honour them now with the dedication of this small volume.

Thank you
to all who made this book possible

In particular John Beauclerk . Adrian Sarin . Colm Connaughton . Rosemary Exmouth . McDavenport of that Ilk . The Duke of St. Albans . Gerard and Carolyn Schurmann . James Warren . John and Valerie Nicholson . Toby Yerborough . Hank Whittemore . Ole Peters . Rachel Grigg . Sally Mosher . Nigel Grant Rogers . Karola Messner . Ana Silva . Susan Campbell . Bonnie Curtin . Christopher Seal . Mildred Sexton . Richard Joyrich . Randall Sherman . Dr David H Goldenburg . Brian Masters . William Ray . John Considine . Dorna Bewley . and all our TPP funders.

Take Physic, Pomp!

WHY THE BOOK?

'For wisdom cries out in the streets and no man regards it'
—Prince Hal, *Henry IV, Part 1.*

'Invest me in my motley. Give me leave
To speak my mind, and I will through and through
Cleanse the foul body of th'infected world,
If they will patiently receive my medicine'
—Jaques, *As You Like It.*

Shakespeare was not only a poet-playwright; he was a sage who saw deeply into human nature and mankind's place in the natural order. He both diagnosed the ills of society—and saw beyond them to a healthier, saner world.

We are living in a society so dysfunctional that an individual with the slightest care for nature, humanity or harmonious living—for sanity in fact—must strike some sort of devil's bargain in order to fit into a system that rewards blindness and is devoid of true sense. People, the earth and all its creatures are being sold for 'a breed of barren metal'. (In the words of Shakespeare, pity has been dispensed with and 'policy sits above conscience.') Finance, fracking, oil drilling, battery farming, consumerism, pointless productivity, corporation-owned governments, wars created by arms companies, technology in service to big business, institutionalized child-abuse—wherever you look cruelty, greed and insanity walk tall, and the fox is firmly in charge of the hen-house. We are poisoning our precious earth and with it ourselves, and in an age of media-drip and quick fixes we appear to lack the introspection to see clearly our originating role in the catastrophic changes currently convulsing the earth. Without this clear-eyed awareness, there is no hope that we will take responsibility, both individually and collectively, for what is happening. How often do we hear, for instance, the self-exculpating lie that global warming has always been with us?

The purpose of this little book is to reveal Shakespeare as philosopher and all-round apothecary of the soul, whose fund of wisdom is there for all human beings to draw from—indeed cries out to be heard. As the Bard himself said, through the lips of King John:

> 'Then pause not; for the present time's so sick,
> That present med'cine must be minister'd.'

Using fifty-two passages from the plays and poems, one for every week of the year, accompanied by their own commentary, the authors show how Shakespeare can help us look at the world with fresh eyes—and timeless wisdom. By linking Shakespeare's words and insights to today's most pressing questions, a dialogue is facilitated between our society and the man Ben Jonson described as 'not for an age, but for all time'. The title of the work is taken from King Lear's speech when he finds himself homeless in the storm. His compassion finally awoken, the king is able to sympathize with his most downtrodden subjects:

> 'Poor naked wretches, whereso'er you are,
> That bide the pelting of this pitiless storm,
> How shall your houseless heads and unfed sides,
> Your loop'd and window'd raggedness, defend you

From seasons such as these? O! I have ta'en
Too little care of this. Take physic, Pomp;
Expose thyself to feel what wretches feel,
That thou mayst shake the superflux to them,
And show the Heavens more just.'
[*King Lear*, 3.4.28-36]

This book is both a journey through the wasteland with our greatest artist as guide and inspiration, and an essential tonic to the soul: for in a world made increasingly barren by mankind's alienation from nature, Shakespeare's words are like healing streams bubbling up from earth's depths.

Take Physic, Pomp!

Lear:

'Take physic, Pomp;

Expose thyself to feel what wretches feel,

That thou mayst shake the superflux to them,

And show the Heavens more just.'

[*King Lear*, 3.4.33-36]

1. TAKE PHYSIC, POMP

What is pomp? The Latin word *pompa* means 'a solemn procession' or 'a train or retinue'; the idea of display and ostentation developed from this primary meaning.

Pomp is variously described in Shakespeare as 'painted', 'absurd', 'dreadful' and 'vain'. It is a sort of vanity and self-importance that signifies loss of empathy. It is the besetting sin of our politicians, who prefer pomp to a frank expression of humanity. Behind it lurks the idea that authenticity is a waste of effort when superiority can be bought so cheaply, and that so long as we can get away with our false words and actions now, we shall never be held to account for them.

King Lear speaks his lines on Pomp at the point at which his compassion awakens and he sheds his self-importance. He knows now that he is only human. Coming from an absolute monarch they are powerful words indeed. 'They flattered me like a dog', he says later. 'They told me I was everything. Tis a lie, I am not ague-proof.'

The leaders of today are time-servers who can only express what is mundane and ephemeral; the eternal, after all, is an obstacle to re-election. Paying mere lip-service to future generations and the fate of the earth, they follow the path of the prince of the world, the master who 'ever keeps a good fire.' The fool in *All's Well that Ends Well* proves wiser than they. 'I am for the house with the narrow gate,' says Lavatch, 'which I take to be too little for pomp to enter.'

Take Physic, Pomp!

'O learn to read what silent love hath writ:
To hear with eyes belongs to love's fine wit.'
[Sonnet 23, lines 13-14]

2. TO HEAR WITH EYES

The overactive life and noisy affirmations of our modern age leave little space for observing and listening to Nature.

If we were to jump off the Ferris wheel of desire and ambition for a few moments every day, we would soon see that Nature expresses herself continually in love: whether it is a tree shedding its leaves or a stream rushing through the woods or the moon casting her beams. Love and being are one in Nature; it is only in man that they have become divided. Love in Nature does not assert itself: it is.

'Love and be silent,' says Cordelia when Lear tries to force his daughters into protestations of love to satisfy his vanity.

Take Physic, Pomp!

Ulysses:

'Take but degree away, untune that string,

And, hark, what discord follows! each thing melts

In mere oppugnancy: the bounded waters

Should lift their bosoms higher than the shores

And make a sop of all this solid globe:

Strength should be lord of imbecility,

And the rude son should strike his father dead:

Force should be right; or rather, right and wrong,

Between whose endless jar justice resides,

Should lose their names, and so should justice too.

Then every thing includes itself in power,

Power into will, will into appetite;

And appetite, an universal wolf,

So doubly seconded with will and power,

Must make perforce an universal prey,

And last eat up himself.'

[*Troilus & Cressida*, 1.3.109-124]

3. UNTUNE THAT STRING

Degree is a key concept, one that Shakespeare understands as intrinsic to the Divine will.

Human greed and ambition—the will to power—have destroyed a sense of connectedness to Nature and with it a consideration of the steps necessary for any kind of life-affirming achievement.

All action is reciprocal and self-reflexive, so when we harm another living thing we harm ourselves. All destruction then can be seen as a form of cannibalism, hence the terrifying crowning image of the universal wolf devouring itself.

Take Physic, Pomp!

Falstaff: 'I will not lend thee a penny.'

Pistol: 'Why then the world's mine oyster, which I with sword will open.'

[*Merry Wives of Windsor*, 2.2.1-3]

4. THE WORLD 'S MINE OYSTER

It is there from the moment you wake in your house with your sheets wrapped around you to the minute you turn off your lamp to sleep in your bed at night. 'The world's mine oyster' is the mantra, the obsession, the desolation.

Shakespeare did not give us the 'world' as our 'oyster'. He gave us 'Pistol', an extravagant fool and cowardly bully who makes a threat when Falstaff refuses to lend him money. Flying into a child-like rage, he asserts that he will take what he wants by force if it is not given, and make it his. In Elizabethan times the Oyster was seen as signifying female parts, and the purity of the Pearl. Add 'sword' to the mix and a picture of rape emerges.

When we realise the world is not a thing to prise open and possess, but our home to cherish and share, we can begin to make amends.

Take Physic, Pomp!

Ariel:

'Where the bee sucks, there suck I

In a cowslip's bell I lie

There I couch when owls do cry.

On the bat's back I do fly

After summer merrily.

Merrily, merrily shall I live now

Under the blossom that hangs on the bough.'

[*The Tempest*, 5.1.88-94]

5. WHERE THE BEE SUCKS

The damage of a calculating educational regime digs its claws into an individual's development, until even as grown-ups we feel guilty unless we can tell ourselves we are using our time productively every waking moment.

Animals—flying, walking, swimming and crawling—find merry joy in the process of a life's work in harmony with the flora and fauna. Our notion of productivity, however, usually involves being destructive to Nature and everything that sustains it and us. No wonder we find it exhausting.

We all suck where the bee sucks. Worthwhile endeavours are the outlaws of modern society's constructions. They do not cost the earth, only require that we treasure our surroundings.

Take Physic, Pomp!

Hamlet:

'The time is out of joint. O cursèd spite,

That ever I was born to set it right.'

[*Hamlet*, 1.5.196-7]

6. THE TIME IS OUT OF JOINT

It is easy for each new age to believe that its problems are both unique and thornier than those of previous generations. But human psychology has not changed over the millennia. We are dealing with the same essential problems as our ancestors, and have the same demons and angels to mediate. Each successive age is 'out of joint'. The only real difference now is that we have the technical ability to destroy the planet we live on. So much more rides on our individual and collective decisions.

We are all microcosms of the universe, so we all have equal responsibility for transforming life on earth for the better through the medium of our bodies, minds and souls. We were all born to 'set the time right' and with the necessary mental adjustment what might have been a 'cursed spite' can become a sacred charge.

Take Physic, Pomp!

Dauphin:

'Thy promises are like Adonis' gardens

That one day bloom'd and fruitful were the next.'

[1 *Henry VI*, 1.6.6-7]

7. ADONIS' GARDENS

The Dauphin's words in praise of Joan of Arc are undercut by a deep irony. What she promised has indeed come about and with miraculous speed, but victory will prove ephemeral. Her inspirations have somehow violated the natural order.

Similarly today, science expects too much of nature, forcing her to flower one day and give fruit the next. This desire to skip the maturing process extends to the way we bring up our children. They are brimful of knowledge, but the emotional life—which requires mulching for the soul's flowers to appear—is neglected. In place of patience we make brave promises. Our children grow up too soon, and their badge is immaturity.

Take Physic, Pomp!

Glendower:

'Why, I can teach you, cousin, to command the devil.'

Hotspur:

'And I can teach thee, coz, to shame the devil

By telling truth; tell truth and shame the devil.

If thou have power to raise him, bring him hither,

And I'll be sworn I have power to shame him hence:

O, while you live, tell truth, and shame the devil!'

[*Henry IV Part 1*, Act 3 Scene 1, 53-8]

8. TO COMMAND THE DEVIL

Glendower is making an outrageous claim. When he says that he can teach Hotspur to 'command the devil', our wise friend implores, 'O, while you live, tell truth and shame the devil!'.

The agglomerated beast of those who attempt to command the devil only to become inveigled into adopting devil-ish ways themselves has made a vulgar mess. The systems and technologies created (often unwittingly) to feed it are reliant upon qualities we have been warned to stay away from in stories passed down through generations, especially in spiritual and religious texts. Those that feature hell as a place you would never wish to visit agree that the devil, his demons, and his demonic powers live deep down within the earth.

Then we drill. We wage wars so often in the name of God, and yet so often in the business of oil—the power that also, as it happens, can be found deep down within the earth. The more we obtain by drilling, the more we discover we need. We become greedy, fearful, lustful, envious. No amount is enough. Drilling turns to fracking in the effort to amass faster, in ways that mean caring less and ruining more. Actual rather than metaphorical fiery furnaces and multiple dimensions of hell are unleashed. We are aware and yet too engrossed to do anything about it. We carry on consuming with unquenchable thirst a fuel that will only ever drive us deeper into the darkness.

All the while, the true heavenly sources of energies we could be cherishing boundlessly await.

Take Physic, Pomp!

'Let me not to the marriage of true minds

Admit impediments; love is not love

Which alters when it alteration finds

Or bends with the remover to remove.

O, no! it is an ever-fixèd mark

That looks on tempests and is never shaken…'

[Sonnet 116, lines 1-6]

9. THE MARRIAGE OF TRUE MINDS

Each time a friendship is formed or a couple commit to wedlock the world is recreated, as it was first created—in the name of love. Time stands still; all obstacles fall away. Truth shakes hands with truth. There is a marriage between the perishable and the immortal.

When Peleus, a mortal, tries to marry the goddess Thetis, she keeps changing shape: fire, wind, water, a tree, a bird, a lion, a tiger, a snake and, finally, a cuttlefish.

Frightened by her metamorphoses, he nevertheless holds her tight until she finally changes back into a woman again. He sees beyond her different forms to the one, essential and transcendent reality.

His mind is true.

Take Physic, Pomp!

'Why should false painting imitate his cheek,

And steal dead seeming of his living hue?

Why should poor beauty indirectly seek,

Roses of shadow, since his rose is true?

Why should he live, now nature bankrupt is,

Beggared of blood to blush through lively veins,

For she hath no exchequer now but his,

And proud of many, lives upon his gains?'

[Sonnet 67, lines 5-12]

10. POOR BEAUTY

To favour an imitation to the detriment of its true form is the misguided preoccupation of society. Many artists and designers create works inspired by the living and natural using production processes that lay waste to the beauty they claim to hold so dear.

The more 'successful' these creators become, the more they make, and the bigger they grow, and the more they need to produce and consume to survive. Their contribution becomes increasingly needy and violent.

Friedrich Nietzsche said that the essence of all beautiful art, all great art, is gratitude. Perhaps the urgent task of the creative is to learn to better give thanks.

Take Physic, Pomp!

Edgar:

'Know my name is lost,

By treason's tooth bare-gnawn and canker-bit.

Yet am I noble as the adversary

I come to cope.'

[*King Lear*, 5.3.143-6]

11. MY NAME IS LOST

In these lines Edgar, who is the hidden prince and godson of the King, expresses his readiness to confront all that is dark and underhand in the state in the form of his half-brother, Edmund. In so doing he acknowledges that he has lost his name or identity, which he describes in royal terms, both as the rose that is canker-bit and the crown that is threatened by treason.

It is not just Edgar's name that is lost, but his rank and reputation. In order to survive the rigours of the state he disguises himself as a lunatic beggar and wanders naked about the countryside. In other words, he puts himself beyond the pale. It is as a madman that he becomes the guide of his blind father.

Today, when the concept of treason appears quaint and irrelevant as applied to the monarch or state, it can still maintain its power and congruity in relation to the human soul. Unless we are prepared to lose our name, just as the Son of Man most far-reachingly did, we cannot come into our true and undivided strength. We shall always be committing treason against the beauty and dynamism of the soul.

Take Physic, Pomp!

Duke Senior:

'Now, my co-mates and brothers in exile,

Hath not old custom made this life more sweet

Than that of painted pomp? Are not these woods

More free from peril than the envious court?

Here feel we not the penalty of Adam,

The seasons' difference, as the icy fang

And churlish chiding of the winter's wind,

Which when it bites and blows upon my body,

Even till I shrink with cold, I smile and say

"This is no flattery; these are counsellors

That feelingly persuade me what I am."

Sweet are the uses of adversity,

Which, like the toad, ugly and venomous,

Wears yet a precious jewel in his head;

And this our life, exempt from public haunt,

Finds tongues in trees, books in the running brooks,

Sermons in stones, and good in everything.

I would not change it.'

[*As You Like It*, 2.1.548-565]

12. TONGUES IN TREES

Duke Senior has been driven into the wilderness. No longer surrounded by pomp, he discovers the medicine of the forest.

The forest as a place of transformation and shelter is the oldest story in the human psyche. It is the rite of passage, where the child disappears and a hero emerges, where the wounded healer discovers a shamanic journey, and where the outlaws regroup away from the prying eyes of the evil king.

Now science confirms that a walk in the woods—or as it is becoming known, 'forest bathing'—can improve our physical and psychological wellbeing, lowering blood pressure and anxiety, strengthening the immune system, and even accelerating recovery from illness or injury.

Surely it is not enough to dip our toes in the water whenever we need a little healing. The forest is more than a plaster to stick over the wounds we gather from destructive ways of life: it is our home.

Take Physic, Pomp!

Olivia:

'Alas, it is the baseness of thy fear

That makes thee strangle thy propriety.

Fear not, Cesario, take thy fortunes up,

Be that thou know'st thou art, and then thou art

As great as that thou fear'st.'

[*Twelfth Night*, 5.1.144-8]

13. FEAR NOT, CESARIO

What is fear but the shadow of our own greatness? We all know the phrase, 'to be afraid of one's own shadow'. It does not simply mean afraid of the darker elements of our natures—our insatiable desires, our viciousness—but afraid too of taking responsibility for the tremendous power (and privilege) that comes with inhabiting a human body. Fear is indeed 'base' because it grows out of a refusal to accept responsibility for our greatness.

Moses asks to see the glory of God, but as He walks by God places his hand over His servant so that he is not destroyed by the sight. Likewise, we are terrified by glimpses of our own potential glory. We prefer to project our greatness onto others, whom we then idolize. When they err, we seem surprised to discover that they are, after all, like us: great perhaps, but human.

Fear makes us lose our self-possession; under its influence we say and do things that are beneath us. Fear is divisive. Clinging to our fragments of knowledge as we do, we see through half-closed eyes, inadvertently dividing the world and ourselves. We forget that the entire universe is within the divine spark that inhabits us. Were this not so, how could we perceive that which is outside us?

Every day brings fresh opportunity for heroism, for putting kindness before mistrust, for banishing fear. 'Be that thou know'st thou art, and then thou art/As great as that thou fear'st'—which is no less than all.

Take Physic, Pomp!

'My mistress' eyes are nothing like the sun;

Coral is far more red than her lips' red;

If snow be white, why then her breasts are dun;

If hairs be wires, black wires grow on her head.

I have seen roses damask'd, red and white,

But no such roses see I in her cheeks;

And in some perfumes is there more delight

Than in the breath that from my mistress reeks.

I love to hear her speak, yet well I know

That music hath a far more pleasing sound;

I grant I never saw a goddess go;

My mistress, when she walks, treads on the ground:

And yet, by heaven, I think my love as rare

As any she belied with false compare.'

[Sonnet 130]

14. MY MISTRESS' EYES

Are we able to view the world unfouled by expectations, and competitions? Can we still look in the mirror and see a reflection, instead of a shifting stereotype—whatever character we wish or fear to become?

We cannot *not* compare. Without differences between things everything would be a great blurry mass. But to compare things unfavourably with things they cannot be is to risk missing out on beauty that may be, in its truth, ever more extraordinary.

Take Physic, Pomp!

Othello:

'Then must you speak......of one whose hand,

Like the base Judean, threw a pearl away,

Richer than all his tribe...'

[*Othello*, 5.2.344;347-9]

15. A PEARL

Othello has thrown away Desdemona, who was quite literally his better half—the purer, gentler, peace-loving, more reflective element of his nature. It was a Judas-like act, not only because of the quality of what he rejected, but because of the betrayal involved: in his case, self-betrayal. Instead of meeting the challenge of greater self-awareness by embracing his feminine nature, Othello falls back on what is familiar and flawed, i.e. the traditional view of what constitutes manhood and honour. He does not have the strength and vision to leapfrog the old Adam.

Thus it is that he disposes of a pearl 'richer than all his tribe.' Shakespeare has chosen his words carefully, for it is the tribe, with its deep-rooted survival instincts and fear of the unfamiliar, that Othello reverts to. In killing Desdemona for honour's sake, Othello buries his individuality in the grave of tradition. The pearl—alas!—was his soul, and we have been re-enacting the murder of Brabantio's daughter ever since.

Take Physic, Pomp!

Timon [looking on the gold]:

'O thou sweet king-killer, and dear divorce

'Twixt natural son and sire, thou bright defiler

Of Hymen's purest bed....................................

....Thou visible god,

That sold'rest close impossibilities,

And mak'st them kiss; that speak'st with every tongue,

To every purpose. O thou touch of hearts,

Think thy slave Man rebels, and by thy virtue

Set them into confounding odds, that beasts

May have the world in empire!'

[*Timon of Athens*, 4.3.384-6; 389-95]

16. THOU BRIGHT DEFILER

Timon, having exiled himself from Athens, has gone to live in the woods. He is digging for roots to eat when he comes upon gold instead—gold that has been the glory and bane of his life. As he knows to his cost, the yellow god distorts relationships between humans, sows mistrust, breaks harmony with Nature: it is the kiss of death to man's integrity.

Its intrinsic worth, like that of money, for which it stands in the play, is zero.

We have become perverted and our money-worship is the surest sign of this perversion. It is a deviancy from Nature that has wrought in us an insatiable wanting and scheming, for which money is the symbol. It has led us not to democracy, but a brutal corporate empire. Maybe we need a word to replace tired old, much abused 'democracy'. How about 'cosmocracy', meaning government in accord with universal Nature? It sounds grand, but would mark a move to conscious simplicity. As D.H. Lawrence wrote in his poem 'Kill Money':

> 'We must have the courage of mutual trust.
> We must have the modesty of simple living.
> And the individual must have his house, food and fire
>   all free like a bird.'

Take Physic, Pomp!

Amiens:

'Under the greenwood tree

Who loves to lie with me,

And turn his merry note

Unto the sweet bird's throat,

Come hither, come hither, come hither.

Here shall he see

No enemy

But winter and rough weather.'

[*As you Like It,* 2.5.1-8]

17. UNDER THE GREENWOOD TREE

We have only just begun to realise how alive the forest is. Trees join beneath the ground through their roots and, with magical sugar-loving fungus, create communication networks. They look after each other, feed their young, and send out messages of warning if they are under attack. They even share information about cures and protections. They mourn and send legacies to eachother when they die. Overground, tree-friends considerately share space, and leave gaps in the forest ceiling to guide saplings to sunlight. They can taste and smell and possess other dimensions of sense we can only begin to dream of. Trees communicate with the creatures that transport their seeds and live within their barks and boughs. They talk to us too, sometimes through pheromones and scent signals.

Just as we have our favourite trees, perhaps they have their favourite walkers. That sigh of welcome on the breeze, the rustle of the leaves that seems so like an invitation, might not be in your imagination after all.

Take Physic, Pomp!

Brutus:

'Ever note, Lucilius,

When love begins to sicken and decay

It useth an enforced ceremony.

There are no tricks in plain and simple faith...'

[*Julius Caesar*, 4.2.19-22]

'

18. NO TRICKS

When true cordiality no longer flows between beings, love is replaced by courtesy or 'ceremony'. Our relationship with Nature is a good example of this. We keep Her at arm's length with words like 'environment' and 'ecology' and promise to increase Her value to society. Beneath this ceremony lies a sinister reality.

The word 'environment' fosters the idea that Nature is something outside us and that we can therefore harm Her without harming ourselves. Not true! Our human nature and the nature outside us are one and the same. Harm one, harm the other. The forest is the steward of the earth's water, hence the religious awe (both wonder and terror) it used to command in the hearts of men. It is one of the gods of our earth. But man has a genius for banishing the divine, and no amount of Facebook posting or twittering can bring it back.

Grimm's fairy tales remind us that the forest is a place of enchantment, the cradle of self-renewal where we come face to face with unconscious images of our deepest being. So, let us lay aside our tricks and get back to a plain and simple faith in Nature, and with it the uncalculating language of the heart. For, she is our mother, not an ill-mannered aunt. In the words of William Wordsworth:

> 'The world is too much with us; late and soon,
> Getting and spending, we lay waste our powers:
> Little we see in Nature that is ours;
> We have given our hearts away, a sordid boon!'

Take Physic, Pomp!

Juliet:

'What's in a name? That which we call a rose
By any other name would smell as sweet.'

[*Romeo and Juliet,* 2.2.43-44]

19. BY ANY OTHER NAME

Juliet is grappling with the problem that Romeo's name makes him an enemy. Romeo then reasons that he will conveniently change it to 'love' instead. As we know, this denial did not end well.

A BBC article from August 2019 claims that the language of Nature is being hijacked by technology. It reported that words such as 'tweet', 'cloud', and 'stream' are used more in the context of the so-called high-tech devices than their original namesakes. Branding enables products to be aligned with familiar sensations that feel good and so attract us to them, regardless of their real impact or what they truly are. At the same time, the declining use of words actually describing Nature—such as blackbird and shell— reflects our withdrawal from the natural world. The piece reported that amongst young people some words, such as 'bumblebee,' had disappeared altogether.

It has not taken a name-change to separate the rose from its sweet smell, only mass production. The market has preferred size, colour and longevity, and so the scent of the rose— with its ability to reduce stress and lower the heart rate—is slowly fading.

Take Physic, Pomp!

Florizel:

'From my succession wipe me, father; I

Am heir to my affection.'

Camillo:

'Be advis'd.'

Florizel:

'I am: and by my fancy. If my reason

Will thereto be obedient, I have reason;

If not, my senses, better pleas'd with madness,

Do bid it welcome.'

[*The Winter's Tale*, 4.4.481-6]

20. BY MY FANCY

Florizel's father King Polixenes has declared he will alienate his son from the succession if he continues in his love for Perdita, thought to be a shepherd's daughter. Florizel's response makes it clear how little he values cold reason, bedfellow of power and tireless prop of misgovernment.

Reason as the master of imagination rather than its servant is a betrayer of the soul. Madness is indeed preferable to such reason. (The Latin word *ratio* from which our 'reason' derives has as its primary meanings 'reckoning, account, and calculation' followed closely by 'plan, scheme and transaction.')

Shakespeare's word 'fancy', on the other hand, beautifully captures the synergy of love and imagination, twin elixirs of our fallen world. Where reason fragments and divides, imagination and love make whole. They are like the leap of the salmon—an embrace of the mystery that is our own exterior depth. Both confirm the truth of our dreams; both require tremendous courage. As Harold Clark Goddard transcendently observed, 'Imagination is the illusion that nothing can shatter.'

Take Physic, Pomp!

Richard:

'I wasted time, and now doth time waste me;

For now hath time made me his numb'ring clock:

My thoughts are minutes; and with sighs they jar

Their watches on unto mine eyes, the outward watch,

Whereto my finger, like a dial's point,

Is pointing still, in cleansing them from tears.'

[*King Richard II,* 5.5.49-54]

21. HIS NUMB'RING CLOCK

Do the processes and technologies claiming to help us manage our time—to free us up—really give us more than they take away?

Our instincts would be able to show us that the palace of efficiencies we have built around us is a prison, but we gag them and shackle them to its bars. As the system hunts down and smothers curiosity, we learn to dread Time rather than treasure it. Still, no matter how misused, stolen or bargained away Time may be, he remains waiting to share with us his unpossessable and priceless nature—the jail-maker's truncheon or a pathway to the infinite.

Take Physic, Pomp!

Helena:

'I know I love in vain, strive against hope;

Yet in this captious and intenible sieve

I still pour in the waters of my love

And lack not to lose still. Thus, Indian-like,

Religious in mine error, I adore

The sun that looks upon his worshipper

But knows of him no more.'

[*All's Well That Ends Well,* 1.3.196-202]

22. THE WATERS OF MY LOVE

How easy it is today to give in to bitterness and hatred, especially when we divide the world into peoples, classes, nations, and religions.

If like Helena, however, we keep pouring in the waters of our love, however unlikely that that love will be returned, we witness something miraculous: our love proves inexhaustible. More than that, the inner well from which it springs can find a sister source outside, helping provide what the world so sorely lacks: fountains of life-giving water.

These holy wells, which it is in all of us to create, are each one linked to the next, like a shimmering necklace of pearls—to make the world one again.

Take Physic, Pomp!

Ulysses:

'One touch of nature makes the whole world kin,

That all with one consent praise new-born gawds,

Though they are made and moulded of things past,

And give to dust that is a little gilt

More laud than gilt o'erdusted.'

[*Troilus & Cressida*, 3.3.175-9]

23. ONE TOUCH OF NATURE

Psychologists of the 1950's worked out how to hack into our brains, deceiving the happy hormone, Dopamine, to reward us with pleasure for buying and consuming new things, whether or not we needed them. The trick relied on gloss and glamour packaged up to seduce us into believing that material gains could fulfil our deep unconscious desires.

Your life is a mess? Have this new gadget, or garment, or game. It will make you feel wonderful. Feeling bad again? Have another. Throw that old one away. The next big thing! On sale! A Bargain. Now, there is no need to leave the house to satisfy your consumer-hit addiction. Stay in bed. Go online, and, 'quick buy', 'quick buy', 'quick buy.' Redefine yourself at the click of a button. The true costs? Hidden, so you do not need to worry about them.

Our weakness for the new is not new itself. It goes back to Eve and the apple. We were never able to tear ourselves away from the promise of shiny new novelty, even at the cost of paradise.

Take Physic, Pomp!

Salisbury:

'The king hath dispossess'd himself of us:

We will not line his thin bestainèd cloak

With our pure honours, nor attend the foot

That leaves the print of blood where'er it walks.'

[*King John,* 4.3.23-26]

24. THE PRINT OF BLOOD

Salisbury speaks for the nobility in condemning King John following the death of his nephew, Prince Arthur. Honour and the shedding of blood are irreconcilable. There no such thing as an honour killing, for honour is harnessed to purity and integrity and is directed at all times by that peerless charioteer, Conscience.

Today Commodity parades himself on the stage of the world and would surely be seen for what he is, were it not that we persist in camouflaging him by lining his threadbare cloak with our 'pure honours'. In other words, we play games with our consciences. Flattered by the crown he wears, we avert our gaze from his bloody footprints.

Yet to live with honour means to defy kings—the more vehemently the more they promise.

Take Physic, Pomp!

Mistress Quickly (as the Fairy Queen):

'Corrupt, corrupt, and tainted in desire!

About him, fairies; sing a scornful rhyme;

And, as you trip, still pinch him to your time.'

The Song:

'Fie on sinful fantasy!

Fie on lust and luxury!

Lust is but a bloody fire,

Kindled with unchaste desire,

Fed in heart, whose flames aspire,

As thoughts do blow them, higher and higher.

Pinch him, fairies, mutually;

Pinch him for his villainy;

Pinch him and burn him and turn him about,

Till candles and star-light and moonshine be out.'

[*The Merry Wives of Windsor,* 5.5.91-103]

25. PINCH HIM

Politics has become a comedy of errors deliberately orchestrated to distract, divide and diminish us, and to shake our focus from the crucial opportunity to work heroically together to establish a better future.

The responsibility of people given the power to make decisions that will define the wellbeing of the living, now and in the future, should be sacrosanct. It should be entirely unthinkable for such a person to tell lies for their own gain, especially to the detriment of the people, creatures and places they are entrusted to care for. To do so should be classed as a most serious offence, with a long jail term for convictions and stripping of the riches amassed as a result of the crime. Just imagine how quickly corruption would vanish.

Take Physic, Pomp!

Orsino:

'O, when mine eyes did see Olivia first,

Methought she purged the air of pestilence.

That instant was I turned into a hart,

And my desires, like fell and cruel hounds,

E'er since pursue me.'

[*Twelfth Night,* 1.1.19-23]

26. TURNED INTO A HART

Orsino idealizes Olivia as the object of his love. It is a mental love, a form of projection that creates a world of shadows and beguiling illusions. Turn over the coin, however, and one sees the dark obverse of such idealism. Shakespeare has Orsino compare himself to Actaeon the hunter who, having been turned into a stag by the goddess Diana, was pursued to death by his own hounds. If the mind lords it over the blood with its beautiful illusions, the blood rises up in retaliation.

Coining false gold (by compulsively idealizing), the mind turns usurer, multiplying frail pleasures at will. Today, the mind harnessed to the Internet proliferates this idealization to a kaleidoscopic degree. Obversely, the Earth—our common body—already in high rebellion, is convulsed to the core by shattering quakes.

'The soil/ Is bare now, nor can foot feel, being shod,' writes Gerard Manley Hopkins in his poem 'God's Grandeur.' Earth and Heart: is there a difference? Let us love like Viola, with the heart; not like Orsino, with the mind. That way we touch the Earth and in touching heal.

Take Physic, Pomp!

Theseus:

'Lovers and madmen have such seething brains,

Such shaping fantasies, that apprehend

More than cool reason ever comprehends.

The lunatic, the lover, and the poet

Are of imagination all compact…………..

The poet's eye, in a fine frenzy rolling,

Doth glance from heaven to earth, from earth to heaven;

And as imagination bodies forth

The form of things unknown, the poet's pen

Turns them to shapes, and gives to airy nothing

A local habitation and a name.'

[*A Midsummer Night's Dream*, 5.1.4-8; 12-17]

27. LUNATIC, LOVER, AND POET

We live in a secular society. What happens, then, to imagination which, as Shakespeare points out, must converse with the divine? Can imagination exist in a secular society? Or must we conclude that no amount of secularization on the part of media-led governments can eradicate the numinous particle in man? Of Shakespeare's three carriers of imagination, only the lover has found a place in our society. The lunatic and the poet are driven to the margins with the sins of society heaped on their backs.

We live in a secular society, where the Unconscious is portrayed as a boiling lake of dragons beneath us. But it is also the heaven above us. It is the ever-living stream of stories, like our blood. Without imagination we cannot live on this earth as human beings. Without imagination the phones that we clutch to our ears and palms will shrink and reappear under our skin.

Without imagination, we shall become metal men, and sooner than we think. Servants of the machine. Without imagination we shall give up the fight to be individuals.

Take Physic, Pomp!

Hamlet:

'I have heard of your paintings well enough. God has given you one face and you make yourselves another. You jig and amble, and you lisp, you nickname God's creatures and make your wantonness your ignorance. Go to, I'll no more on 't. It hath made me mad.'

[*Hamlet,* 3.1.144-9]

28. WANTONNESS YOUR IGNORANCE

Why do we have to scribble our insecurity over everything? Preoccupation with ownership creates only ruin. We cover rich nutritious earth with concrete, replace trees with sky-scrapers, and rivers with roads. As for the great gift, a glimpse of the universe, soon we will not even be able to look upon the same night-sky as our ancestors, or tell a star apart from an internet-beaming satellite. How could we cover such beauty with such ugliness?

All an individual can truly possess is their own perspective—the unique experience of their life as lived by them. Is this not enough?

Take Physic, Pomp!

First Lord:

'The web of our life is of a mingled yarn, good and ill together; our virtues would be proud if our faults whipp'd them not, and our crimes would despair if they were not cherish'd by our virtues.'

[*All's Well That Ends Well,* 4.3.68-71]

29. A MINGLED YARN

What is conscience? Is it there to distinguish between right and wrong? Yes or no, conscience never used to have a moral dimension; it had the larger meaning of 'consciousness' or 'common knowledge' in the sense of what man collectively knew. The narrower moral sense can be dangerous in that it encourages us to reject parts of our nature that society deems unacceptable. Then our striving to be better becomes totalitarian and unnatural and calls forth the very forces that we demonize.

In *The Art of Growing Old* the novelist and sage John Cowper Powys wrote, 'If by the time we are sixty we haven't learned what a knot of paradox and contradiction life is, and how exquisitely the good and bad are mingled in every action we take, we haven't grown old to much purpose.'

Take Physic, Pomp!

Duke:

'How shalt thou hope for mercy rend'ring none?'

Shylock:

'You have among you many a purchas'd slave,

Which (like your asses, and your dogs and mules)

You use in abject and in slavish parts,

Because you bought them,—shall I say to you,

Let them be free, marry them to your heirs?

Why sweat they under burthens? let their beds

Be made as soft as yours, and let their palates

Be season'd with such viands? you will answer

"The slaves are ours,"—so do I answer you:

The pound of flesh which I demand of him

Is dearly bought, 'tis mine and I will have it:

If you deny me, fie upon your law!'

[*The Merchant of Venice*, 4.1.88-101]

30. THE POUND OF FLESH

Antonio, who like Shylock is a rich merchant, has shown no sympathy or understanding towards the Jew or Jewish culture in general during the course of the action, nor have his aristocratic friends. Indeed, they have evinced considerable hatred. On the other hand, Shylock refuses to accept their hospitality and says of Antonio, 'I hate him for he is a Christian.' When asked by the Duke why he is not merciful towards Antonio but insists instead on his pound of flesh, Shylock points out that the Duke and his Christian brethren keep slaves; indeed, it is the foundation of the Venetian economy and they would not dream of treating them mercifully.

Shylock has a point. Each culture has its own blind spot. We are all hypocrites in some regard, such is the complexity of our modern world. For instance, we may condemn slavery in all its forms and yet own hi-tech gadgets such as iPhones made in factory compounds in China, where the conditions are often so inhuman as to cause epidemics of depression and suicide among the workers.

It is too easy to paint the world in terms of black and white. That is the path of fundamentalism. Indeed, all racism is based on a misperception. No one is black and no one is white; we are all combinations of the two both physically and in our souls—hence the reality of the shadow in psychology. The only way to remove hypocrisy and racism from the world is to acknowledge our own shadow. Only in perceiving our own darkness will we cease to judge others.

Take Physic, Pomp!

Coriolanus:

'What custom wills, in all things should we do't,

The dust on antique time would lie unswept,

And mountainous error be too highly heap'd

For truth to o'er-peer.'

[*Coriolanus,* 2.3.125-8]

31. DUST ON ANTIQUE TIME

Even when we think we are innovating, as in the case of technology, we are more often than not doing no more than following custom or conventional thinking. Our novelties are merely the latest fashion, possessing little or no originality. (Custom is strongly allied to the word 'costume'. At root, it is about fashion and presenting a face to the world.)

Too much custom, Shakespeare avers, is the enemy of truth. It can accumulate in our lives and before we know it we have built a wall of error, over which we cannot peer. It can dull us both to the beauty around us and to our own destructive ways. It can kill our culture. Hamlet refers to 'that monster, custom, who all sense doth eat/ Of habits evil.'

Intuition, on the other hand, breaks down the wall of unknowing, for with intuition (from the Latin *intueri,* 'to look upon'), seeing and knowing are one. Such knowledge comes from deep within and does not rely on the vision of others.

At the end of *King Lear*, Edgar enjoins us to 'speak what we feel, not what we ought to say.' Today, drowning as we are in an endless whirlpool of collective opinion, this is more difficult than it sounds—and more vital than ever!

Take Physic, Pomp!

Caliban:

'You taught me language; and my profit on't

Is, I know how to curse. The red plague rid you

For learning me your language!'

[*The Tempest,* 1.2.366-8]

32. I KNOW HOW TO CURSE

In his essay 'Politics and the English Language' George Orwell wrote, 'If thought corrupts language, language can also corrupt thought.' He called politics a 'mass of lies, evasions, folly, hatred, and schizophrenia,' and his description of 'various tricks' to dodge the work of prose construction includes the use of stale metaphors, pretentious diction, and meaningless words.

Is Caliban implying that Prospero's language has corrupted his thoughts, leading him to curse? Or has the language shown him a world he feels needs cursing?

Aimé Césaire in his retelling of *The Tempest* wrote these raw new words of Caliban:

> 'Prospero, you are the master of illusion.
> Lying is your trademark.
> And you have lied so much to me
> (Lied about the world, lied about me)
> That you have ended by imposing on me
> An image of myself.
> Underdeveloped, you brand me, inferior,
> That's the way you have forced me to see myself
> I detest that image! What's more, it's a lie!
> But now I know you, you old cancer,
> And I know myself as well.'

Perhaps the idea of becoming civilised is the true corrupter.

Take Physic, Pomp!

Duke of Albany:

'That nature, which contemns it origin,

Cannot be border'd certain in itself;

She that will sliver and disbranch

From her material sap, perforce must wither

And come to deadly use.'

[*King Lear*, 4.2.32-6]

33. TO DEADLY USE

Nature is not only our mother, but our guru. Her roots are in the divine, and drink from founts of silent wisdom. We are the flame-like shoots and branches of her universal tree. When we are born we enter into a sacred marriage with her and, being part of her tree, stand like Yeats's sages 'in God's holy fire'. Our blood family, its stories and rituals, are as ever-living leaves on Nature's tree; as are the members of our spiritual family, the shining spirits of the past who have taken human form and the conductive spirits of animals who send their starry messages from beyond the temporal frame.

When we divorce ourselves from Nature, however, as we are now recklessly doing, and break off from the universal tree, the life passes out of us. We become the living dead. No longer fed by our material sap, we graft ourselves instead to an artificial tree whose only soil is the endless fussy commentary of other human beings. We are uprooted in the profoundest sense, and compassion dies on the vine.

Take Physic, Pomp!

Constance:

'You have beguiled me with a counterfeit

Resembling majesty, which, being touch'd and tried,

Proves valueless: you are forsworn, forsworn;

You came in arms to spill mine enemies' blood,

But now in arms you strengthen it with yours:

The grappling vigour and rough frown of war

Is cold in amity and painted peace,

And our oppression hath made up this league.'

[*King John,* 3.1.25-32]

34. COUNTERFEIT RESEMBLING MAJESTY

Just as we have time-honoured memories, wisdoms, fables and heroes to act as shining guides through dark and trying days, there are also dressed-up tales, so often delivered as news, covertly designed to enervate the mind and distract us into acting in a way that is not our natural state. These lesser stories beguile us by tapping into our most fearful and insecure traits. Instead of teaching us to look within, they enrage us. They provoke us to give our energies to letting anger build over manufactured misunderstandings and misleading information between people who would otherwise be friends. Then, when we turn upon eachother, we allow oppression and inequality to reign. The real monsters can continue to wreak destruction, while we are engrossed in their diversions.

'Divide and conquer' is a military strategy for achieving—or sustaining—political or military control. We should better recognise when it is being used against us.

Take Physic, Pomp!

Duke of Albany:

'If that the heavens do not their visible spirits

Send quickly down to tame these vile offences,

It will come,

Humanity must perforce prey on itself,

Like monsters of the deep.'

[*King Lear,* 4.2.46-50]

35. MONSTERS OF THE DEEP

Albany prays for an influx of divine energy or a collective shift in consciousness to prevent the destruction of human-kind. Such is the harrowing millenarian vision of *King Lear*. We too are living at a time that has the feel of 'end days', when only a massive change in perception among humankind (a wrenching of the frame of Nature) can prevent savagery from breaking out on a global scale. As for the false prophets predicted by Jesus, they are ten a penny, though they charge heavily for their bouquets of wisdom.

Ironically, the very technology that was meant to liberate us has enslaved us. More than that, it has made us deeply unconscious. Until schools teach the most vital thing of all—how to take responsibility for one's emotional life, so that it doesn't spill out into the world and generate violence *hic et ubique*—then we shall continue to spin round on the wheel of fortune without any control over our lives. Like the alchemists of old, we must use our monsters (our primordial passions) to transform ourselves, not unleash them on others.

If we don't actively engage in this opus, we will become those monsters. All plans, however ingenious, will prove futile, and what appears to be a new order will simply turn out to be a further degree of disorder.

Take Physic, Pomp!

Henry VI:

'Thou never didst them wrong, nor no man wrong;

And as the butcher takes away the calf

And binds the wretch, and beats it when it strays,

Bearing it to the bloody slaughter-house,

Even so remorseless have they borne him hence;

And as the dam runs lowing up and down,

Looking the way her harmless young one went,

And can do nought but wail her darling's loss,

Even so myself bewails good Gloucester's case…'

[*2 Henry VI*, 3.1.209-17]

36. CAN DO NOUGHT BUT WAIL

Industrial farming—increasingly referred to as the animal holocaust—will come to be known as one of the worst crimes in history. What kind of a world do we live in, where ripping the beaks off birds and the tails off cows can be called a job? Where somebody has spent precious time designing a machine to shred chicks alive? Where tiny cages are manufactured for the affectionate pig to spend a lifetime in, driven to madness? The mother cow forcibly impregnated for milk still wails for days for the young calf torn away from her and often in much sadder conditions than she would have endured in Shakespeare's era. As these words are being written, millions upon millions of sentient beings are suffering terribly in sunless concrete places and will be brutally killed having never known a moment of peace or kindness. Surely it stands to reason that (just as when we spray poison on plants and then eat them, we too will be poisoned) if we poison creatures, physically or psychologically, and then devour them we will find their pains within us? How would we change our ways if sentenced to re-live the life of each creature whose skin or meat we will consume? Why do we persist in treating other beings in ways we would hate to be treated ourselves?

In the 6th Century BC, Pythagoras said that, 'as long as Man continues to be the ruthless destroyer of lower living beings, he will never know health or peace. For as long as men massacre animals, they will kill each other. Indeed, he who sows the seed of murder and pain cannot reap joy and love.'

Will we never learn?

Take Physic, Pomp!

Bishop of Ely:

'The strawberry grows underneath the nettle,

And wholesome berries thrive and ripen best

Neighbour'd by fruit of baser quality:

And so the prince obscur'd his contemplation

Under the veil of wildness; which, no doubt,

Grew like the summer grass, fastest by night,

Unseen, yet crescive in his faculty.'

[*Henry V*, 1.1.60-66]

37. UNDER THE VEIL OF WILDNESS

It was at the Bishop of Ely's house in London that John of Gaunt—'a prophet new inspir'd'—made his visionary speech describing England as 'this blessed plot.' The Bishop of Ely's gardens were known to produce the finest strawberries in the capital. Richard III saw them on a visit there and requested Ely to send him a batch. The strawberry, a member of the Rose family, is unique in that it is the only fruit with seeds on the outside. It wears its heart on its sleeve. A symbol of healing and rebirth, it is the first fruit to ripen in the spring.

Here the Bishop of Ely and Archbishop of Canterbury are discussing Prince Hal's sudden transformation from prankster to statesman. Ely understands that it has been a process of maturation and that Hal has used his tavern companions as a 'veil of wildness,' trusting to the alchemy wrought by his proximity to these vital, if indiscriminate forces. Similarly, the strawberry is known to grow with peculiar vigour in the shade of the nettle, strewing itself best at night when the sun is absent.

We live in a one-sided, overlit world. Anything that smacks of death, decay, darkness, wilderness or inactivity is demonized as harmful and contrary to the modern ethos of unrelenting growth and happiness. We are, alas, no longer open to the moon's soothing embrace. Even the healing power of the body itself has been supplanted by the concocted brain of computer technology. Not long now and our 3-D printers will press out reams of strawberries patterned after Othello's fatal hanky.

Take Physic, Pomp!

'Since brass, nor stone, nor earth, nor boundless sea
But sad mortality o'er-sways their power,
How with this rage shall beauty hold a plea,
Whose action is no stronger than a flower?
O, how shall summer's honey breath hold out
Against the wrackful siege of batt'ring days,
When rocks impregnable are not so stout,
Nor gates of steel so strong, but time decays?
O fearful meditation! where, alack,
Shall time's best jewel from time's chest lie hid?
Or what strong hand can hold his swift foot back?
Or who his spoil of beauty can forbid?
O, none, unless this miracle have might,
That in black ink my love may still shine bright.'
[Sonnet 65]

38. NO STRONGER THAN A FLOWER

Is there a way to save seemingly fragile beauty in the face of impermanence? How poignant it is, that because of his own mortality the author would never know whether his miracle held true.

A tree can rise for hundreds of years only to be felled by a storm or an axe in a matter of hours. It might seem that the storm or the axe has the upper hand. But then, look longer. The noise disappears and the forest, with the knowledge of that tree within its roots, is still standing. That was how Nature, and the Human within Nature, worked. Now, with our Machines of Death unleashing unnatural violence—too much, too fast—the balance is breaking.

In Mayan times, the flower was used as a symbol of life and fertility. What better contrast could there be to wanton destruction? In an image entitled 'The Ultimate Confrontation: the flower and the bayonet', a woman holds a chrysanthemum up to an approaching wall of gun-clad soldiers, and we clearly see which is the true force. When a light is shone, darkness has to fade. Flower-power, instigated by a poet in 1965 as an antidote to violence, might not have stopped the Vietnam war; but decades after that particular battle has gone, a voice still rings out over the airways: 'All you need is love.' Love, like the flower, endures.

Take Physic, Pomp!

Touchstone:

'Why, thou sayest well. I do now remember a saying,
The fool doth think he is wise, but the wise man
knows himself to be a fool.'

[*As You Like it*, 5.1.29-31]

39. THE WISE MAN KNOWS

Thinkers throughout the centuries have puzzled along these same lines, going all the way back to Confucius who said, 'to know is to know that you know nothing.' More recently, a man robbed two banks with his face covered in lemon juice—believing it would act as invisible ink and hide his identity from the cameras. Subsequent experiments by David Dunning and Justin Kruger of Cornell University led to the Dunning-Kruger effect that states, 'If you're incompetent, you can't know you're incompetent.… [T]he skills you need to produce a right answer are exactly the skills you need to recognize what a right answer is.'

What if human civilisation was built with this condition as the fault-line running through it? Incompetence—in the guise of right answers—passed down and exacerbated by each generation? How could we know that we really know anything? As Rumi said, 'Sell your cleverness and buy bewilderment. Cleverness is mere opinion, bewilderment is intuition.'

Take Physic, Pomp!

Timon:

'And, in some sort, these wants of mine are crown'd,

That I account them blessings.'

[*Timon of Athens,* 2.2.191-2]

40. BLESSINGS

Can there ever be a spiritual economy on earth, one where wants are not perceived as wants? From the moment we are born we are taught to condemn want and suffering as wrong and many dedicate their adult lives to fighting these 'evils'. But as soon as we label experiences negative, we cease to see which way they point. More than that, we lose the divine thread of our lives and with it any sense of individual destiny. We place ourselves at the mercy of chance. Refusing such judgments, however, creates a breathing space for life to work its magic unencumbered.

Fairy tales, those baffling flowers of the unconscious (in which deprivations are crowned), teach us that life on earth is a testing-ground, and meaning the lamp that lights our path through the hazardous dichotomies of good and bad, light and dark. Meaning is the ultimate token of God's love and presence, and it is through faith that we touch and are touched by meaning. Padre Pio wrote, 'What does it matter to you whether Jesus wishes to guide you to Heaven by way of the desert or by the meadow, so long as He is always with you?'

Uniquely among the animals, man has been given the power to bless. So let us bless, and bless wisely!

Take Physic, Pomp!

'I, from the orient to the drooping west,

Making the wind my post-horse, still unfold

The acts commenced on this ball of earth.

Upon my tongues continual slanders ride,

The which in every language I pronounce,

Stuffing the ears of men with false reports.

I speak of peace while covert emnity,

Under the smile of safety, wounds the world…'

[*2 Henry IV,* induction, lines 3-10]

41. THE SMILE OF SAFETY

How safe can we really be? After all, we're all going to die in the end. Laws created to prevent danger have reduced many untimely deaths, but how often can a promise of safety be used as a decoy to stifle and control? As we wade through mountains of paperwork to prove that we ourselves are operating safely, mass annihilation thunders along unchecked.

A cook wishing to make a living in a village by serving wholesome meals will jump through hoops for the required certificate to do so. All the while, supermarket food produced for millions is lawfully laced with poisons. Leaving a dog in a car on a hot day will rightly lead to an investigation for cruelty, yet factory farming is left untouched.

The whims of the corporation ride roughshod over the logic of the human, often under the guise of keeping us safe. In a world in which fracking is allowed, and the climate (and pretty much everything else) is breaking down because of our ways, the authenticity of the Health and Safety dictatorship should surely be called into question. Do we submit, and become safe soldiers of our own suffocation? The words of Charlie Chaplin spring to mind, 'We might as well die as go on living like this.' Accepting false security at the price of liberty is surely a most reckless act. Better to take a risk in sowing the seeds of freedom.

Take Physic, Pomp!

Claudius:

'Now, Hamlet, where's Polonius?'

Hamlet:

'At supper.'

Claudius:

'At supper! where?'

Hamlet:

'Not where he eats, but where he is eaten. A certain con-vocation of politic worms are e'en at him. Your worm is your only emperor for diet. We fat all creatures else to fat us, and we fat ourselves for maggots: your fat king and your lean beggar is but variable service—two dishes, but to one table. That's the end.'

Claudius:

'Alas, alas!'

Hamlet:

'A man may fish with the worm that hath eat of a king, and eat of the fish that hath fed of that worm.'

Claudius:

'What dost thou mean by this?'

Hamlet:

'Nothing but to show you how a king may go a progress through the guts of a beggar.'

[*Hamlet*, 4.3.17-31]

42. WHERE HE IS EATEN

It is a cliché that we are all food for worms. By intricate and never-ending processes of transmutation everything in the universe permeates everything else. It is a physical—and therefore a psychic—law. We are one.

In an age of body culture and fitness fanaticism, where respect for health and the body descends into the realm of vanity and its underlying fears, we seem intent on providing the worms with a very expensive banquet indeed. On the other side of the coin, chronic obesity and population explosion worldwide are furnishing our limbless invertebrate friends and all Nature's waste-disposal workers with more than they can consume.

There are ways, however, to make human involvement in these processes less onerous to the earth. For a start, we were never meant to eat other animals; that is not a dignified thing for the stewards of the earth to be doing. In the very first chapter of Genesis we have, 'And God said [to Adam and Eve], Behold, I have given you every herb bearing seed, which is upon the face of all the earth, and every tree, in which is the fruit of a tree yielding seed; to you it shall be for meat.' Secondly, we would do well to simplify our diet until it has the feel of a sacrament, and eat only what is in season locally.

Carnivorousness in humans changes Nature's attitude to us, as well as ours to Her. We become predatory (and less able to breathe the ether that will one day be our most refined food), thus allowing the human story to be arrested in an ever-recurring cycle of pleasure and pain.

Take Physic, Pomp!

Isabella:

'And the poor beetle that we tread upon

In corporal sufferance finds a pang as great

As when a giant dies.'

[*Measure for Measure,* 3.1.78-80]

[The authors wish to acknowledge that although they may appear to have taken this particular passage from Shakespeare out of context, the playwright often undercut the meaning intended by a character—in this case the unsympathetic Isabella—with another sense in keeping with a deep and humane vision.]

43. THE POOR BEETLE

Without empathy we would be unable to understand or relate to anything outside ourselves. We would be completely alone all of the time. To feel how others feel, whether they be beetles or giants, and to realize that others can feel as we do, is surely the greatest gift to humanity, and of life. To connect with all the worlds around us is our freedom and our beauty.

But then, just as the feeling of being at one with another is to find heaven, to feel the pain of another is akin to hell. Nobody wishes to face that. But in place of the giant of yore who could feel the misery of the beetle and act accordingly, we have created an altogether unfeeling giant—the corporation, the system, the machine—which without the capability of caring for anything other than its own business works to destroy our innate sympathies.

The tools to which we are addicted are working at the expense of everything natural and good in this world. We are increasingly programmed to conform, creating a superficial unity that is light years away from empathy. Politically acceptable subjects are bandied about divisively, whilst other crucial issues are just as divisively overlooked.

Our first responsibility must be to the 'earthlings' that share this planet with us. When we undermine them, we diminish ourselves as well.

Take Physic, Pomp!

Friar Lawrence:

'These violent delights have violent ends

And in their triumph die, like fire and powder

Which, as they kiss, consume.'

[*Romeo and Juliet*, 2.6.9-11]

44. VIOLENT DELIGHTS

We are each a miracle and we come from a world that is made of good, yet collectively we seem to build around ourselves fetid palaces of death. The way we treat everything is completely baffling. From childhood we naturally cheer for and fall in love with the fairy-tale brave hero, the beautiful heroine and their magical friends. How, then, do we grow up to take on the shape of the monster more destructive than anything a story could invent? We eat the dead, dress ourselves in the dead, build houses made of and containing dead things, and we warm and power ourselves with oily rivers formed from layer upon layer of death. Spoon-feeding death into each aspect of life, we become truly grisly creatures.

How did this deadly thanatocracy come about? If we spend time surrounded by wildlife, we might arrive at the same conclusion as the water wizard Viktor Schauberger who, within his process of 'comprehend and copy nature,' realised that our technological systems follow the same explosion principle Nature uses for decay (death) rather than implosion, which is the pattern for creation (life). He said, 'In every case do the opposite to whatever technology does today. Then you will always be on the right track.'

Take Physic, Pomp!

Jaques:

'Invest me in my motley. Give me leave

To speak my mind, and I will through and through

Cleanse the foul body of th'infected world,

If they will patiently receive my medicine.'

[*As You Like It,* 2.7.58-61]

45. INVEST ME IN MY MOTLEY

The fool's motley was a badge of honour in Shakespeare's eyes, for the court jester was the truth-teller. An outsider with no standing, his task was to rail at pomp in all its manifold forms and disguises. He spoke his mind without fear of retribution, and his trenchant wit—rooted in the healing genius of the unconscious—was the perfect physic for the ills and folly of the court. He was the very antithesis of the status quo.

Our world is 'infected' as much by our thoughts as our deeds, and we seem to have little patience for understanding. We have abused our beautiful earth, denuding her forests, polluting her oceans, drilling her for oil, blasting and mining her for precious minerals, and now fracking her for gas. The mind that can justify such activities without heed to their disastrous repercussions for both nature and humanity is sick indeed.

Shakespeare's medicine was art, which helps re-forge our broken bonds with nature. Again and again he comes before us in the guise of the fool, the joker, the wild card, the man from left field, the innocent—the true hope of humanity.

Where is the jester today?

Take Physic, Pomp!

Salisbury:

'Therefore, to be possess'd with double pomp

To guard a title that was rich before,

To gild refined gold, to paint the lily,

To throw a perfume on the violet,

To smooth the ice, or add another hue

Unto the rainbow, or with taper-light

To seek the beauteous eye of heaven to garnish,

Is wasteful and ridiculous excess.'

[*King John,* 4.2.9-16]

46. TO PAINT THE LILY

'Consider the lilies of the field, how they grow; they toil not, neither do they spin: yet I say unto you, that even Solomon in all his glory was not arrayed like one of these.' Jesus' words remind us that Nature is a portal to a transcendent realm. It is not a treasure-house to be plundered, nor is it a second-rate work of art that requires improving. It asks only two things of humanity: stewardship and wonder. To these it opens its doors.

Our culture today is defined and dictated to by ridiculous and wasteful excess…twisted pictures of perfection produced in increasingly destructive ways. Even our lifestyles are mass produced to follow a paradigm that paints and stifles rather than celebrates and treasures the lily. All the while true beauty is to be found outside these bars.

This division of man and Nature has made life tremendously complex and tremendously superficial. It has had a devastating impact on the arts, which are increasingly noisy and sensationalist. Even Shakespeare, whose works like Rembrandt's spiral inwards towards silence, must be dolled up to keep pace with modern life. Depth, alas, holds out his tattered hat at street corners.

Take Physic, Pomp!

Macbeth:

'Will all great Neptune's ocean wash this blood
Clean from my hand? No, this my hand will rather
The multitudinous seas incarnadine,
Making the green one red…'

[*Macbeth,* 2.2.59-62]

47. ALL GREAT NEPTUNE'S OCEAN

Earlier in the play Lady Macbeth had said, 'A little water clears us of this deed'. Her husband is wiser and knows that his crime, the murder of a king, has a universal quality and cannot be absolved by washing his hands in the sea. Rather, the blood of the murdered king will turn all the oceans red.

At a time when humankind has created suffering and havoc in Nature on an unprecedented scale, it is essential to ask ourselves how our accumulated sin can be purged and redeemed. Or are we destined to keep turning the oceans and rivers red until we destroy both the earth and ourselves?

Hercules tried to clean out the Augean Stables (with their piled-up muck of decades) using a shovel, but soon realized that he would barely make a hole in it if he continued shovelling for the rest of his life. So he diverted the course of two rivers instead and that way washed the stables clean.

'I am the world and the world is me,' said Krishnamurti. Macbeth understood this, but didn't act on his understanding. He could have washed away his sin, but it would have required a complete change of perception—the creation of a new channel of energy such as Hercules created by diverting the two rivers. In murdering the king, Macbeth killed his own soul.

Whatever the spin doctors might say, there is a huge price for human sin—one that not only we pay—and our pitiful lack of moral imagination is blocking the wellspring of absolution.

Take Physic, Pomp!

Richard II:

'...for within the hollow crown

That rounds the mortal temples of a king

Keeps Death his court, and there the antic sits,

Scoffing his state and grinning at his pomp...'

[*Richard II,* 3.2.160-3]

48. THE HOLLOW CROWN

Death is the ultimate jester (or 'antic') because He is the truth-teller that cannot be contradicted. He is the dark mirror. We all die; everything passes. The great temples and palaces, the frail achievements of humanity, all fall to ruin. Nothing living is exempt from the law of Death.

Yet do we not spend most of our lives pretending He is not there?

Death mocks pomp because it is created in defiance or denial of His inexorable law. If we were to become more conscious of Death in all our dealings, not only would our wisdom and peace of mind increase, but so would the beauty and vitality of the world. Our rulers would renounce their worldly power for something deeper, more cooperative, and Nature would recognize in us a kindred spirit.

We come into this world naked, and naked we depart. The closer we are to that state, psychologically speaking, by the time we die, the better; looking back, the second half of life will be seen to have been a kind of stripping bare of all that is not us. The Hindu knows this, for the greatest teacher in the Upanishads is Yama, King of Death.

Take Physic, Pomp!

Antonio:

'Mark you this, Bassanio,

The devil can cite Scripture for his purpose.

An evil soul producing holy witness

Is like a villain with a smiling cheek,

A goodly apple rotten at the heart:

O, what a goodly outside falsehood hath!'

[*Merchant of Venice,* 1.3.92-7]

49. THE DEVIL CAN CITE SCRIPTURE

We live in a relentlessly superficial world. Everything is about appearance and 'perception'; how a person presents or markets himself has become paramount—how he sells himself, one could say. What he is remains hidden.

Our TV culture, which extends to all areas of public life, is one of fake smiles and false jollity; seriousness is devalued and derided as 'uncool', while every day we are exhorted to 'chill out', 'lighten up' and 'keep it sweet.' But why do we need to be upbeat all the time? Does the sun shine every day? Why can't we simply be ourselves?

The politicians and religious leaders who preach love and do evil are easy to recognize; they fool no one. Much more dangerous because pervasive and anonymous is the average man who has swallowed the poisonous diet of collective consent and chumminess. 'What a nice fellow!' we might be tempted to exclaim, because his lack of depth and reality preclude the possibility of true communion. Spending time with him is as anodyne as watching telly. He smiles and smiles, and all the while the anger is putrid in his soul.

Beware the smiling saint! There are countless false prophets today, most of them smiling. They are decidedly 'cool.' They tell us that we can grow spiritually without pain or suffering; their words soothe us. All we need do is smile and repeat a few affirmations before breakfast and the world will be saved. They look so appealing and make it seem so easy and comfortable. Yet it is all false. They sit upon their anger, smiling.

Take Physic, Pomp!

Menas:

'We, ignorant of ourselves,

Beg often our own harms, which the wise powers

Deny us for our good; so find we profit

By losing of our prayers.'

[*Antony & Cleopatra,* 2.1.5-8]

50. BY LOSING OF OUR PRAYERS

All too often our prayers are no more than veiled wishes and, not knowing ourselves, we wish for our own harm. But if we put aside our wishes and prayers, a deeper listening can take place and with it a deeper harmony with all that surrounds us.

St. Paul in *1 Thessalonians* (5.16) enjoins us to 'pray without ceasing.' He follows this by saying, 'In every thing give thanks,' which gives us a clue as to how to interpret the former injunction. Paul is talking about a state of mind in which we cease to ask for anything, but instead look at the world through the eyes of gratitude.

Take Physic, Pomp!

Hamlet:

'There are more things in heaven and earth, Horatio,

Than are dreamt of in your philosophy.'

[*Hamlet,* 1.5.167-8]

51. THINGS IN HEAVEN AND EARTH

When we look outside ourselves to the universe, it is easy to become baffled, or even frightened, by its sublime greatness. We glimpse the fragility of everything, and face how briefly we will be alive. As the profound mysteries occur to us, challenging us to see past our mortal situations, it is all too easy to look away and become busy with building ordered predictable constructs that make us feel safe and reassured.

The intrepid travellers, however, willing to boldly traverse the existential states may find themselves gazing into the eyes of the Almighty only to discover their own true selves reflected. As Friedrich Nietzsche said, 'You must have chaos within you to give birth to a dancing star.'

Take Physic, Pomp!

Helena:

'I am not an impostor, that proclaim

Myself against the level of my aim,

But know I think, and think I know most sure,

My art is not past power, nor you past cure.'

(*All's Well that Ends Well*, 2.1.154-157)

52. NOT PAST CURE

Helena trusts that she can cure the King of France, despite his pompous dismissal of her claim, because she trusts in the power that works through her. She knows that she will hit the target even before she has taken aim. She could have let self-doubt assail her and ruin her perfect aspiration, but she chooses instead to believe in her original vision of a healed human, holding to her ideal in the face of scorn and disbelief.

If we humans never allow the ideal in our hearts to trump reality, then our future can only be disease and death. After all, it is the imagination that connects us with all that is most magical, which—paradoxically—is all that is most real. 'He who does not imagine in stronger and better lineaments and in stronger and better light than his perishing and mortal eye can see,' wrote William Blake, 'does not imagine at all.'

So let us believe together in the power of imagination to heal the world and administer to pomp its lethal dose, leaving to Shakespeare himself—our imperishable seer—the final word:

'All's well that ends well yet,
Though time seem so adverse and means unfit.'

Take Physic, Pomp!